DK LIFE Stories

BARACK OBAMA

DK

LIFE Stories

BARACK OBAMA

by Stephen Krensky

Illustrated by Charlotte Ager

Senior Editor Marie Greenwood
Designer Brandie Tully-Scott
Editor Niharika Prabhakar
Project Art Editor Kanika Kalra
Art Editor Mohd Zishan
Publishing Co-ordinator Issy Walsh
Jacket Designers Brandie Tully-Scott, Dheeraj Arora
Jacket Illustrator Alessandra De Cristofaro
DTP Designers Dheeraj Singh, Vikram Singh
Picture Researcher Aditya Katyal
Production Editor Abi Maxwell
Production Controller Leanne Burke
Managing Editors Jonathan Melmoth, Monica Saigal
Managing Art Editors Diane Peyton Jones, Ivy Sengupta
Delhi Creative Heads Glenda Fernandes, Malavika Talukder
Deputy Art Director Mabel Chan
Publishing Director Sarah Larter

Subject Consultant David C. Barker
Literacy Consultant Stephanie Laird
Sensitivity Reader Bianca Hezekiah

First published in Great Britain in 2022
by Dorling Kindersley Limited
DK, One Embassy Gardens, 8 Viaduct Gardens,
London, SW11 7BW

The authorised representative in the EEA is
Dorling Kindersley Verlag GmbH. Arnulfstr. 124,
80636 Munich, Germany

Copyright © 2022 Dorling Kindersley Limited
Text copyright © 2022 Stephen Krensky
A Penguin Random House Company
10 9 8 7 6 5 4 3 2 1
001–331882–Sept/2022

A CIP catalogue record for this book
is available from the British Library.
ISBN: 978-0-2415-6989-4

Printed and bound in China

For the curious
www.dk.com

Dear Reader,

In 2009, history was made when Barack Obama became the first African American president of the United States.

A man of huge ability, warmth, and natural charm, Barack grew up in the sixties and seventies, a period of great change in the US. By nature, Barack was practical and grounded, but he had a hopeful streak as well. Barack saw clearly that some things in the United States were wrong and needed to be addressed, but he also believed firmly that this fixing could be done. As his life unfolded, he kept looking for platforms where he could do more and more good for more and more people.

The presidency was the ultimate platform, and from there he accomplished a great deal. And he is not done yet. While the presidency is now behind him, he remains a force for good — an example for helping Americans become what Abraham Lincoln once called "the better angels of our nature".

Happy reading!
Stephen Krensky

The life of...
Barack **Obama**

An **unsettled boyhood**

Barack Obama was born in 1961 – at the start of a decade that marked a turning point for civil rights in the United States.

At that time the United States remained a segregated country. Prejudice against African Americans was widespread. In some states Black people could not use certain hotels and restaurants, and Black children had to attend separate schools. Black adults were not allowed to hold many professional jobs. Even public toilets and drinking fountains were segregated.

SEGREGATION

Segregation is the act of separating people into different groups for the purpose of treating them differently. In the case of racial segregation, this unfair separation is based on skin colour.

DRINKING FOUNTAIN
WHITE   COLORED

Drinking fountain sign showing segregation.

Many people of all races took part in protests and demanded change. They wanted African Americans to be treated fairly. This campaign for social justice and equal rights for African Americans was called the Civil Rights Movement.

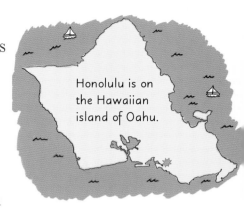

Honolulu is on the Hawaiian island of Oahu.

In the middle of this turmoil, Barack Hussein Obama made his first appearance into the world on 4 August in Honolulu, Hawaii. Barack's parents, Barack Obama Sr and Ann Dunham, met at the University of Hawaii while taking a Russian language course. Their romance was a little unusual for the time – with widespread racism and laws upholding segregation, it was uncommon to see a Black man and white woman holding hands.

Baby Barack Obama

what is turmoil?   A period of unrest or great uncertainty.

Ann's parents, however, were open-minded enough to accept Barack Sr into their home and their family.

The idea that Barack Sr and Ann could then marry was also not something to take for granted. Interracial marriage was forbidden in many states, but luckily Hawaii was not one of them.

When baby Barack, or Barry as he was called, was two, his father received an offer for graduate work at Harvard University in Cambridge, Massachusetts. This was exciting news for Barack Sr, who was eager to continue his education. However, the offer only provided enough money for him to make the trip by himself. Ann agreed to the move even though she was worried about the idea of their being so far apart.

"In many parts of **the South,** my father could have been **strung up from a tree** for merely looking at my mother the **wrong way.**"

Barack Obama

So Ann and Barry stayed in Honolulu with her parents, but, as she had predicted, the 8,000-kilometre (5,000-mile) distance made things difficult. Two years after Barack Sr moved to Cambridge, the couple broke up and decided to get a divorce.

Young Barry was not too negatively affected by the split though, and continued to have a happy childhood. His mother and grandmother took care of him, and he spent his days playing outside in the park or going to the beach.

Years later, Barack described how he could still "retrace the first steps I took as a child and be stunned by the beauty of the islands. The trembling blue plane of the Pacific. The moss-covered cliffs. The North Shore's thunderous waves, crumbling

Barack (far right) with his mother Ann, his half-sister Maya, and his stepfather Lolo.

as if in a slow-motion reel. The shadows off Pali's peaks; the sultry, scented air."

Before long, Barry was introduced to a new man in his mother's life. This was Lolo Soetoro, a visiting student from Indonesia. Barry enjoyed spending time with Lolo. When his mother told him that she and Lolo were going to get married, Barry didn't mind at all.

And in 1966, when Lolo learned that he had to return home, Ann made plans for her and Barry to follow him.

Indonesia was a new world for them. The capital, Jakarta, made a strong first impression on Barry. The roads were filled with many cars, rickshaws, and overcrowded buses. At their new home, Barry found chickens, ducks, birds of paradise, a cockatoo, and two baby crocodiles.

There were new eating experiences as well. Barry tried raw green chilli peppers and he later described tasting "dog meat (tough), snake meat (tougher), and roasted grasshopper (crunchy)... One day soon, [Lolo] promised, he would bring home a piece of tiger meat for us to share."

Although Barry went to school with the local children, his mother Ann was keen for her son to have the very best education possible.

Early each morning she spent three hours teaching him English so that he would read and write fluently. When Barry protested, she often reminded him by saying, "This is no picnic for me either, buster".

Looking back, Barry was grateful for his mother's high standards. And as he got older, she came to realize that, as much as they appreciated Indonesia, she believed that his chances for a better life lay elsewhere.

And so it was time to go home to Hawaii.

2

A **bittersweet** return

**Ten-year-old Barry Obama was more
than a little nervous. It was his first day
at Honolulu's private Punahou School.**

Barry didn't know any of the other kids,
and his classmates saw him as the new boy
from Indonesia. Although he was born in
Hawaii, Barry hadn't grown up with any
of his classmates and he felt left out. Most of
Barry's classmates had much in common, since
"they lived in the

Punahou School

neighbourhoods, in split-level homes with swimming pools; their fathers coached the same Little League teams; their mothers sponsored the bake sales".

Meanwhile, Barry was now living with his grandparents in their two-bedroom apartment. (His mother and little sister Maya were still in Indonesia, living with Lolo.)

Barry stood out as one of the few African American children enrolled in the school. Nobody there played soccer or badminton or chess, which were Barry's favourite things to do. Also, he had no clue of how to do the things the other children cared about, "to throw a football in a spiral or balance on a skateboard".

A year later, his mother Ann and his sister Maya returned to Hawaii.

Lolo was not with them, though, because he and Ann had grown apart.

Although Barry's mother was no longer teaching him lessons, she continued with Barry's moral education. She had strong feelings about the way human beings should treat each other. She was against "any kind of cruelty or thoughtlessness or abuse of power, whether it expressed itself in the form of racial prejudice or bullying in the schoolyard or workers being underpaid". She also encouraged Barry to take great pride in his racial heritage.

It was around this time that Barry's father made an unexpected visit. Barack Sr had not been back to Hawaii for eight years. After finishing at Harvard, he had begun working for the government in Kenya. However, he was now recovering from having been badly injured in a car accident. The visit had many awkward moments.

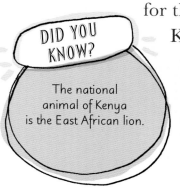

DID YOU KNOW?

The national animal of Kenya is the East African lion.

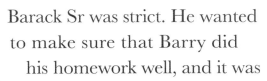

Barack Sr was strict. He wanted to make sure that Barry did his homework well, and it was hard for Barry to live up to his father's many expectations. Barack Sr had one other important thing in mind. He wanted Ann, Barry, and Maya to return with him to Africa. In Kenya, Barack Sr already had two wives and six children. The practice of having more than one partner, called polygamy, was perfectly legal, but Ann was not interested in joining such an extensive family. She refused the offer.

A few years later, Ann finished her graduate work and made plans to return to Indonesia. She expected Barry to go back with her and

---

what is polygamy?

This is the practice, which exists in some societies, of marrying more than one partner, often in the same household.

Maya. But he said no. The idea of starting
all over again didn't appeal to Barry at all.
Besides, he had already spoken to his
grandparents, and they had agreed that
he could live with them.

Part of the deal with his grandparents
was that Barry would cause no trouble.
For a typical teenager this was sometimes
easier said than done. Barry went through
the same awkward teenage stages as everyone
else. His mind and body were both growing,
but not always in sync with each other.

Barry's passion over the next few years was
basketball. He loved the game, spending hours
and hours passing balls, taking jump shots, and
perfecting a crossover dribble. He went onto
play for the Punahou high school team. "Barry
O'Bomber" he was called at school for his
jump shot.

However, not everything was as simple
as trying to score a three pointer. Barry was
still trying to work out exactly who he was.
He developed a rebellious streak, and invented

Barack playing basketball at high school.

reasons to argue with his grandparents.

But by his senior year in high school, Barry had matured. He had realized that starting arguments for the sake of arguing wasn't very fulfilling. He may not have recognized himself as getting older and wiser, but he was doing it just the same.

"I started to appreciate his need to feel **respected** in his own home. I realized that **abiding by his rules** would cost me little, but to him it would **mean a lot.**"

Barack Obama, about his grandfather

Chapter 3

From **coast to coast**

In the autumn of 1979 Barry went to Occidental College in Los Angeles, California. This was a big step for Barry.

Although California is the nearest state to Hawaii, it was still far from home and Barry was going to be living away from his family for the first time. However, Barry adjusted to life at college well enough. He went to class, ate in the dining hall, and hung out with his friends. Barry enjoyed socializing with students from

Barack travelled 4,000 km (2,500 miles) from Hawaii to California.

Barack at Occidental College in 1980.

many different countries and from diverse ethnic backgrounds.

When talking with his Black friends, Barry realized how different his childhood experience was from theirs. Hawaii was far less discriminatory than other US states, and along with his middle class background, Barry had a more privileged upbringing than many other Black students. This new awareness made him begin to think a lot about civil rights.

As Barry met and had conversations with more young Black people, they talked about how upsetting it was to be discriminated against.

They discussed how racism was embedded in society, how parts of society were set up to exclude them. It was harder for Black people to get high paying jobs, good places to live, and even things like good medical care. Barry and his friends realized they wanted to change the ways society was unfair.

Eventually, Barry became involved in the issue of civil rights in South Africa. In this country, a system called apartheid kept Black and white people segregated, and Black people had far fewer rights.

At one campus rally, Barry spoke about divestment in South Africa. This involved people boycotting, or refusing to support, any

APARTHEID AND DIVESTMENT

Apartheid was the system of discrimination against Black people in South Africa from 1948 until 1994. Protesters from other countries demanded that international companies stop operating in South Africa until apartheid was overturned. If these companies refused, then, campaigners argued, people should no longer support them. This was called the divestment campaign.

company that still did business there. Apartheid wasn't overturned until 1994 – 13 years after Barry graduated – but being involved in the divestment campaign made him realize he could be part of a bigger cause.

The audience was moved by Barry's speech. It meant a lot to him, realizing the impact his words could have. Feeling empowered and encouraged, Barry decided to make some personal changes. He knew the time had come to leave the name Barry behind. His name was Barack, and he should be proud of it.

The new Barack decided to make a fresh start. He transferred to Columbia University

DID YOU KNOW?

Columbia University was founded in 1754 as King's College, when New York was still ruled by a British king.

in New York City. He knew that there he would find a larger Black community, one that was more diverse.

Both Columbia and New York were overwhelming in many ways – bigger, more intense, but in some ways more dreary than Los Angeles. Barack took months to adjust to his new setting. He also became a more serious student, learning about social injustice and pursuing a major in political science.

Columbia University in New York City

While at Columbia, Barack received some terrible news from Kenya. His father had died, killed in a car accident. He was only forty-six. Barack had been planning to visit his father in the near future. Sadly, that reunion would no longer be possible.

Barack Obama Sr

As Barack approached graduation in the spring of 1983, he decided to become a community organizer. Such a job would give him the chance to improve the conditions of city people who lived in underprivileged communities.

COMMUNITY ORGANIZERS

Community organizers usually work for a non-profit agency that is not part of local government. Their job is to help residents resolve problems that affect their daily lives. While these are not the problems that necessarily make headlines, they are still important. They might include fixing broken streetlights or improving the safety standards in apartment blocks.

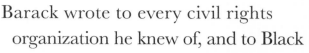

Barack wrote to every civil rights organization he knew of, and to Black officials around the country. But no one even answered his enquiries. Stuck for the moment, he accepted a more conventional job doing research for a company that assisted American firms operating abroad.

As the months passed, and he succeeded at work, his views softened. It became tempting to think of building a corporate career that would earn him lots of money, even though this would not be helping people directly, as he had wanted. What shattered this plan was more bad news from Kenya. His younger half-brother David had died.

Jolted from his comfortable cocoon, and with a new perspective on life, Barack quit his job and decided to go back to the community work he loved. He renewed his search for a position as an organizer, taking on a few temporary assignments along the way, such as encouraging recycling and passing out flyers for a political race. But after six months, he was broke and hungry. Was it possible, he wondered, to find a meaningful job that also paid the salary he was dreaming of?

And then he got a call from Chicago.

4

Community organizer

**Barack had been to Chicago once before.
As a ten-year-old boy, he had visited the city
with his mother, grandmother, and sister, Maya.**

However, the city had changed since then,
electing Harold Washington as its first Black
mayor. Even so, the effects of segregation were
still visible. Many African Americans who had
moved to Chicago from the South in the
previous decades were living in poor housing
conditions. This created
racial tensions that
were not going away
any time soon.
Barack's job was
with the Developing
Communities
Project, a

church-based community organization. His boss was a white organizer who had hired him for a practical reason – he needed a Black man to work directly with the Black community. Barack would assist unemployed workers on Chicago's South Side, trying to help them find new jobs. He would also search for general grievances to air. These might be neighbourhood or housing development issues. Barack started out by introducing himself at local meetings. He interviewed anyone who was willing to speak to him. At first, nobody trusted him. Gradually, after months of hard work,

DID YOU KNOW?

Chicago's South Side historically contained some of the poorer and more dangerous parts of the city.

he came to be accepted. The more experience he got, the more he learned about these people's backgrounds. Many of them were from Chicago, but wherever they were from, they were used to oppression. Being considered second-class citizens no longer surprised them, since it had been their way of life for so long. They did not believe that change was possible, and it left the whole community feeling worn down.

Barack's early work focused on a public housing project called Altgeld Gardens.

Graffiti art at
Altgeld Gardens,
Chicago.

The inhabitants there were so used to the disappointments of daily life that they had lost even the strength for outrage. Barack later noted, "The drive-by shootings, the ambulance sirens, the night sounds of neighbourhoods abandoned to drugs and gang war... – none of this was new. In places like Altgeld, prison records had been passed down from father to son for more than a generation... "

Barack had some success over the next three years, but he came to realize that complicated issues couldn't be solved simply by untangling some political red tape or putting pressure on a lazy city agency. In the high schools, for example, many students were dropping out, often giving up on life before they had even started, or turning to illegal activities to make ends meet.

How did people face such overwhelming barriers without getting crushed? Some drew great strength from their religion, and Barack envied them. He was the first to admit that he had no such anchor. His father had been raised a Muslim and his mother a Christian. But neither one had been religious as an adult. His mother's decision to remain apart from the Christian Church had suited her particular sense of independence. But in Chicago, Barack saw how a strong church created a supportive community. He missed that sense of belonging.

So Barack was delighted to discover a church where he felt at home. The revelation surprised him. It surfaced when he heard a sermon at the Trinity United Church of Christ. The sermon was called "The Audacity of Hope", and it brought Barack to tears.

Stained glass windows, at the Trinity United Church of Christ, in Chicago.

Hope was not about logic or practicality. Hope was an ideal, fed by faith. It could be beaten down, it could be delayed, but it could never be entirely erased.

Such thoughts encouraged him to take the next step forward. A community organizer could only do so much. Barack wanted to do more.

Law school seemed like the logical next step. A few months later, he was accepted by Harvard Law School in Cambridge, Massachusetts, one of the most prestigious law schools in the country.

Harvard Law School,
Cambridge, USA

Barack realized that there was always some danger in taking the road to advancement. He might be tempted to leave the fighting to others. Why not be satisfied with being a good example, a shiny role model? He could work in the right firm, live in the right neighbourhood, and make the right donations to the right causes.

DID YOU KNOW?

Among Harvard Law School's distinguished graduates were several Supreme Court Justices.

However, he had faith he would find a different path. With luck, "the audacity of hope" would be his guide.

5

A trip to Kenya

It was the summer of 1988, and Barack was looking forward to starting law school in the autumn.

However, first he wanted to go to Kenya and meet some of his family there.

In truth, Barack was a little nervous about making the trip. What if somehow the reality was different to the ideal?

Nairobi, Kenya

What if he didn't measure up? What if he found himself disappointed with the place itself?

When Barack arrived in the capital, Nairobi, he found himself staring at pieces of history mingled together. Old buildings stood side-by-side with modern high-rise offices and elegant shops. This pattern of old and new showed up everywhere.

Barack's guide was his half-sister, Auma, whom he had met in Chicago when she visited there. As well as showing him the city, Auma gave Barack a more complete picture of their father.

The "Old Man", as she called him, had experienced a dramatic rise and fall in the Kenyan government. He was smart and dedicated, but refused to play the political games necessary to stay in power.

"I am telling you, his problem was that his heart was too big," she said. "When he lived, he would just give to everyone who asked him. And they all asked."

It was also an adjustment for Barack to meet his big and extended family. He met his stepmother, Kezia – his father's first wife, and the mother of Auma. He met Kezia's sister, Jane. He also got to know his half-brothers and lots of cousins and other relatives spanning

Barack with his family: front row (left to right): Auma (Barack's half-sister), Kezia (Barack's stepmother), Sarah Onyango (third wife of Barack's paternal grandfather), Zeituni Onyango (Barack's aunt). Back row (left to right): Sayid (Barack's uncle), Barack Obama, Abongo (Roy) (Barack's half-brother), unknown woman, Bernard (Barack's half-brother), Abo Obama (Barack's half-brother).

generations. His family, he noted, "seemed to be everywhere: in stores, at the post office, on streets or in the parks, all of them fussing and fretting over Obama's long-lost son".

Barack noticed some familiar sights, too. Aunt Jane's apartment had "the well-worn furniture, the two-year-old calendar, the fading photographs," much like the ones he had seen in Chicago.

Barack's travels took him out into the countryside where the landscape was dazzling. In the Great Rift Valley, he saw "stone and savannah grass stretched out in a flat and endless plain, before it met the sky and carried the eye back through a series of high white clouds". In other places the land teemed with wildlife – herds of zebras and gazelles, lions, elephants, and "wildebeest, with mournful heads and humped shoulders that seemed too much for their slender heads to carry".

DID YOU KNOW?

The Great Rift Valley is home to volcanoes, geysers, and earthquakes.

The Great Rift Valley stretches across East Africa.

The rivers revealed hippos with "pink eyes and nostrils like marbles bobbing on the water's surface". Not every scene was fit for a postcard, though. He also saw hyenas eating wildebeests, "their chins dripping with blood", while "vultures watched patiently from the treetops, waiting for their turn to dine".

One story about Barack's own grandfather sounded like something out of a folk tale: "Once upon a time, a man wanted to pass through Grandfather's land. But Grandfather refused to give permission because he thought the man's goat would eat some of his plants. The man protested. He insisted that his goat

was very well behaved and would eat nothing.
So Grandfather changed his mind – on one
condition. If the goat nibbled at even the
smallest leaf, Grandfather would cut off
its head. The man agreed to this. Surely, he
thought, his goat would behave itself for just
a few minutes. So Grandfather let them pass.

However, the goat had not gone far when
it reached out and bit off part of a leaf. A
moment later, and – whoosh! Grandfather
had cut off the goat's head.

The man who owned the goat was very
upset. How could Grandfather do such a thing
over a small piece of leaf? Grandfather was
calm and confident in his reply. 'If I say

I will do something, I will do it. Otherwise how will people know that my word is true?'"

Stories like these revealed much about Kenya. Values, at least on the surface, can be different from one place to another. But underneath, the universal truths remain.

Barack returned home to America with a lot to think about.

Chapter 6

Law school and **beyond**

When Barack started law school in the autumn of 1988, he already was twenty-seven, older than most of his fellow classmates.

There was nothing particularly unique about Barack as a first-year student. After all, there were other students who were the same age as him, and plenty of students who were inspired to practise law after working for non-profit organizations, just like he had done.

Barack at law school

Then, at the end of his first year, he won a spot, along with 80 law-review editors, supervising the *Harvard*

Law Review. This
important journal was
written by legal scholars
from all over the
country, so this was a
great opportunity.

That summer, Barack
returned to Chicago to work as an
intern, or trainee, for a law firm that worked
with big businesses. Corporate law was not a strong
interest of Barack's – it was a long way from
community organizing – but the position paid well,
and he needed the money to make a dent in his
student loans.

Every intern was supervised by someone
in the firm. Barack found himself assigned to a
young lawyer named Michelle Robinson. Three
years younger than Barack, she had already
graduated from Harvard Law School.

Michelle had heard a lot about Barack even
before they met. Other lawyers in the office
had plenty of nice things to say about his
intelligence, his writing ability, and his good

looks. However, she wasn't intrigued. A specialist in entertainment law, Michelle was intent on putting all her energy into her career.

Barack felt differently. Michelle was an excellent supervisor, but from the moment they met, he hoped for more than a professional relationship. It took Michelle a little longer to return the feeling. Finally, she agreed. On their first date, he took her out for ice cream. They got along very well. At one point, Barack asked if he could kiss her – and, with her permission, he did.

Barack was not only drawn to Michelle, he was drawn to her family, too. As he later wrote,

being around the Robinsons and the home they had made together made him realize something he'd been looking for: a sense of place, of stability, of roots and home.

By the time Barack returned to Harvard in the autumn, he and Michelle had become a couple. They maintained a long-distance relationship filled with late-night phone conversations. Then, Michelle's father died suddenly from complications after a kidney operation. Barack was at her side to comfort her and their love deepened.

Barack continued to dedicate himself to his studies and

Barack and Michelle on a trip to Hawaii, 1989.

51

he ran for president of the *Harvard Law Review*. Some said afterwards that he won because of the sense of fairness he projected. Even when he disagreed with people, he respected their right to have a different opinion. As the first-ever Black president of the *Harvard Law Review*, Barack attracted national attention. Articles about him appeared in major newspapers and magazines. Job offers began to pour in. He could probably have got any position he wanted after graduation.

But Barack remained true to his earlier convictions. After graduating in the spring of 1991, he returned to Chicago to practise civil-rights law. As he described it at the time, "In my legal practice, I work mostly with churches and community groups, men and women who quietly build grocery stores and health clinics in the inner city, and housing for the poor".

His personal life underwent some significant changes, too. On 3 October 1992, he and Michelle were married.

Barack and Michelle on their wedding day, October 1992.

Barack had also begun writing a book about himself – a book that became a memoir, or personal account, of his life. It traced the inner and outer journeys he had travelled on the way to discovering his identity. *Dreams from My Father* was published in 1995. The book was particularly applauded for the honesty with which its author had revealed the circumstances of his life.

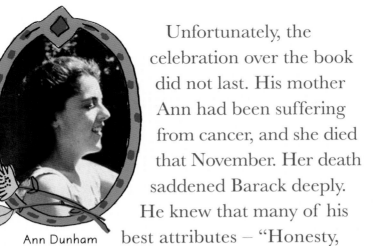

Ann Dunham

Unfortunately, the celebration over the book did not last. His mother Ann had been suffering from cancer, and she died that November. Her death saddened Barack deeply. He knew that many of his best attributes – "Honesty, empathy, discipline, delayed gratification, and hard work" – had come from his mother.

Barack would do his best to uphold the values she had prized the most.

Chapter **7**

Politics beckons

Barack was living the American Dream. He was a happily married newlywed living in a city he enjoyed and doing a job he liked.

He had written a bestselling book about his upbringing, was well-respected by his colleagues, and still enjoyed getting out on the basketball court. However, the 34-year-old lawyer was restless. Something was missing. He was glad to be able to help his clients. But what of those people who never made it to his door? Barack felt it was time to make change happen on a larger scale.

Barack was inspired by the American political

56

South Side, Chicago

tradition, from its roots breaking free of
colonial rule through the momentous changes
of the Civil Rights Movement.

As it happened, there was an opening
for a state senator from Chicago's South Side.
Barack knew the area well and decided to run
for the seat. But who knew what would happen
next? He needn't have worried. Barack brought
his energy and his firm beliefs to the voters –
and they liked what they saw. He was
nominated as the Democratic candidate
and then won the election.

Barack was excited to work in the state
capital at Springfield. However, this new state

US ELECTIONS

US elections to elect a president to lead the country take place every four years.

 Democratic Party: one of the two current major political parties in the United States.

 Republican Party: the other major political party in the United States.

 Primary: an election before the final election to choose candidates to represent a political party.

 State senate: one half of the branch of government in a state that oversees and passes laws for that state.

State legislators: elected officials who write and pass laws on behalf of people they represent in the state where they live.

 US Congress: one of three main branches of the federal government in the United States. It creates the nation's laws for the president to sign.

legislator was only one of many. Nobody was putting him in charge of anything, or even paying much attention to his being there.

Bobby Rush

Barack gained some valuable experience, but at the end of his second two-year term, he decided to run for the US Congress. The congressman who held the job was Bobby Rush. Unlike Obama's first stab at politics, running for an open seat, this time was different. Representative Rush had every intention of holding onto his job. But Barack went ahead anyway.

The campaign did not go well, and Barack lost. "The sort of drubbing that awakens you to the fact that life is not obliged to work out as you'd planned." Temporarily discouraged, he returned to the state senate.

Of course, life was not only about politics. Important changes at home were drawing

Barack Obama on the campaign trail.

more and more of his attention. And this was a good thing. Barack and Michelle's first daughter Malia was born in 1998, and her sister Natasha (called Sasha) followed in 2001. Barack delighted in his daughters and the time he spent with them.

Meanwhile, Barack was continuing to make a name for himself in the state senate. And he made a big impression when he spoke at an antiwar rally in Chicago in 2002.

Barack and Michelle with their daughters, Malia and Sasha.

IRAQ WAR

The war with Iraq began in 2003 with the invasion of Iraq by a group of countries led by the US. The goal was to remove Saddam Hussein as the leader of Iraq and get rid of the "weapons of mass destruction" that were thought to be under his control. No such weapons were ever found, however. The conflict led to unrest in the region that continues to the present day.

A lot of people disagreed with the idea of invading Iraq, a step that seemed likely in the near future. However, Barack wasn't sure the crowd would want to hear what he had to say. As he later told a reporter, "... a lot of people at that rally were wearing badges saying, 'War Is Not an Option'. And I thought, I don't agree with that. Sometimes war is an option." After all, as he had argued in his speech, both the American Civil War and World War II had been worth fighting.

Despite the attention he gained, Barack could not shake the feeling that his career in politics was perhaps permanently stalled.

But before moving on, he considered taking one last chance to move up. A seat for the United States Senate was becoming available in the state of Illinois for 2004. Barack would be an underdog in a crowded field. But he remained hopeful. Michelle – ever watchful of the effect it could have on their growing family – was more reluctant at first. However, she agreed to support him in giving politics one more shot.

"I am **not** opposed to all wars. I am opposed to **dumb wars**."

Barack Obama

8

Going to **Washington**

Seven primary candidates fought for the 2004 Democratic nomination for the United States Senate in Illinois.

Several of them were popular and well connected. And then there was Barack Obama.

As he listened to people up and down the state, he paid close attention. "Most of them," he noted, "thought that anyone willing to work should be able to find a job that paid a living wage... They wanted to be safe, from criminals and from terrorists; they wanted clean air, clean

water, and time with their kids. And when they got old, they wanted to be able to retire with some dignity and respect."

Obama won the primary in March with a decisive 53 per cent of the vote. One person clearly impressed was

Senator John F. Kerry

Senator John F. Kerry of Massachusetts. At the Democratic Convention in July, he was going to be named as the Democratic candidate for president. For four days there would be speeches and more speeches. But the keynote speech was considered very important. It often served as a springboard for a younger politician.

And Kerry chose Obama to give it.

So, on a Tuesday night, in front of thousands of people at the convention itself, and millions more watching on television, Barack Obama spoke up. He touched on his recurring themes, "... that we

What is a convention? A convention is a gathering of people who are meeting to discuss issues of shared interest.

can tuck in our children at night and know that they are fed and clothed and safe from harm; that we can say what we think, write what we think, without hearing a sudden knock on the door... "

In those few minutes Barack Obama went from being an Illinois politician to a major figure on the national stage. On 2 November, George W. Bush was re-elected to a second term as president. But in Illinois, the Democratic candidate for the senate won 70 per cent of the vote. Mr. Obama was going to Washington.

Barack Obama and Republican rival Alan Keyes during a debate.

US GOVERNMENT

The US Government is made up of three equal branches: executive, legislative, and judicial.

The Executive branch, led by the president, administers control over federal laws that govern the whole country.

The Legislative branch is made up of the House of Representatives and the US Senate. They create the laws that govern the country.

The Judicial branch includes the court system, and is overseen by judges who interpret federal laws as needed.

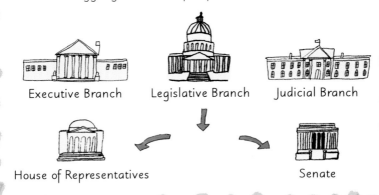

Executive Branch   Legislative Branch   Judicial Branch

House of Representatives   Senate

When he got there in January 2005, he found Republicans in a good mood. President George W. Bush had won re-election, and they had also retained control of both the House of Representatives and the Senate in Congress.

During this time of Republican control, Obama became a rising star for the Democratic Party. One of his greatest hopes was to break down the rigid political walls that kept people bitterly apart. His daily schedule as a senator was filled with meetings and more meetings, speeches and more speeches.

But, however busy he was, Senator Obama often thought of his family. As someone who had grown up without a father in the house, he was determined that his daughters would not feel the same absence. As part of his weekly schedule, he tried to get home to Illinois early enough on Thursdays to put the girls to bed. On Saturdays, he was not a senator – he was a dad and a husband, playing with his children or doing chores like laundry or grocery shopping.

DID YOU KNOW?

The Obamas decided to keep their home in Chicago and not move the family to Washington.

When Senator Obama took office in
January 2005, he planned to serve out his
full term. But over the next year and a half,
he began to change his mind. Senator Hillary
Rodham Clinton of New York was the
early frontrunner for the next Democratic
presidential nomination. A senator for six years,
she was also the wife of former president Bill
Clinton and had served as First Lady for the
eight years of his presidency. Her support cut
across a wide range of Democrats and was

Democratic US Senator Hillary Clinton speaks to a crowd of supporters in 2008.

particularly strong among women. Other people, though, were unhappy at the prospect. They felt that the presidency was beginning to look like a club with only two families as members – the Bush family (George W. Bush's father, George H.W. Bush, had also been president) and the Clintons.

Running for president would be a bold move. However, voters looking for change were drawn to Barack Obama. He got people excited in a way that had not been seen for many years. But not everyone applauded the idea. Had two years in the Senate and a few more at the state level really prepared him for the most difficult job in the world? Even his daughter Malia had asked him: "Are you going to try to be president? Shouldn't you be vice president first?"

The new senator was the first to admit he still had a lot to learn. But he also had a vision of the kind of America he wanted to live in. And Barack Obama was determined to help America get there.

Chapter 9

The **2008 election**

On 10 February 2007, Barack stood in front of a large crowd in Springfield, Illinois to announce his intention to run for President.

This challenge was the biggest political risk Barack had ever taken. However, what set him apart was an articulate presence, a youthful vigour, and an unabashed sincerity. He could rouse a convention hall of thousands and still seem like someone you could have dinner with afterwards.

The passing weeks revealed that Barack was a tireless campaigner. He would rise at dawn to greet factory workers starting their shift and still be working fourteen hours later when giving an after-dinner speech.

DELEGATES

Every state sends delegates, or representatives, to the national political conventions. The number of delegates from each state depends proportionally on the state's population. The larger the population a state has, the more delegates it gets.

Eventually, the nomination came down to a fight between Barack Obama and Hillary Clinton. The two candidates swapped victories in one primary after another. Gradually, though, the momentum – and the lead – turned Barack's way.

In early June, Barack passed the 2,118 delegate mark. This was the number he needed to win the nomination. The race was over.

The Democratic Convention was held in Denver that August. It was there that Barack

DID YOU KNOW?

Obama broke with tradition by accepting the Democratic nomination in an open-air stadium rather than in the usual convention hall.

chose Senator Joe Biden of Delaware, considered an expert on foreign affairs, to be his running mate.

While the Democrats were busy choosing their candidate for president, the Republicans were doing the same. But they quickly settled on their nominee, Senator John McCain of Arizona.

Political observers expected John McCain to pick a vice president from one of the men who had run against him for the nomination. Instead, he surprised friends and foes alike by selecting Governor Sarah Palin of Alaska.

JOE BIDEN

Democrat Joe Biden served in the United States Senate from 1973 until he was elected to be vice president in 2008. He spent eight years in that office. In 2020 he ran for the presidency, and after winning that election, he became president of the United States in January 2021.

John McCain introduces Alaska governor Sarah Palin during a campaign stop in Dayton, Ohio, on 29 August 2008.

Sarah Palin was almost unknown outside of her home state. However, she made a big splash. As a confident, hardworking woman who was an energetic public speaker, she found supporters all around the country.

As the campaign picked up in September, both candidates had to be careful. Senator McCain was a decorated war hero. Certainly, Obama could criticize McCain's views, but he could never suggest that McCain lacked integrity or courage.

The political energy and excitement that Barack Obama sparked had not been seen in decades.

Instead of following the traditional model of creating one group of campaigners and then spreading out in the fifty states, Barack's team built a large campaign group for each state. The money he collected and the volunteers he led both dwarfed John McCain's efforts.

It was widely recognized, though, that Barack Obama had no political experience in foreign affairs. Given ongoing American concerns about terrorism from abroad, John McCain seemed to have the advantage.

But then the economy fell. Actually, it had been falling since the spring, like a balloon that

What is an economy?

An economy is the wealth and resources of a country, including the buying and selling of everything from goods to services.

had sprung a slow leak. But in September, the balloon just popped. The stock market plunged, and huge companies were suddenly at risk of shutting down. Hundreds of thousands of people were losing their jobs each month.

Senator McCain hurt his own cause by insisting that the economy was still in good shape. Barack, in contrast, projected a sombre awareness of how serious this crisis was. If elected, he was prepared to take whatever steps were necessary to solve it.

On Election Day, 3 November, Barack Obama voted in Chicago, and then waited for the results to come in. Just after 11 pm in the east, the news outlets declared Barack the winner.

People get in line to vote in the 2008 Presidential election.

Barack Obama with his wife Michelle and their daughters Sasha (left) and Malia on the stage of his election night victory party in Chicago's Grant Park.

After midnight, Barack Obama stood before a huge crowd in Chicago's Grant Park and shared his thoughts.

He thanked the crowd for their support and pledged to lead not some of the people, but all of the people going forward into his presidency. It was truly a night to remember.

"In this country, we rise or fall as **one nation**, as **one people**. Let's resist the temptation to fall back on the same partisanship and **pettiness** and **immaturity** that has poisoned our politics for so long..."

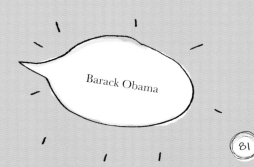

Barack Obama

Chapter 10

President Obama

On Inauguration Day, 20 January 2009, President Barack Obama was sworn into office and gave his inaugural address.

Every elected US president gave a speech after taking the oath of office. The speeches didn't necessarily have much in common. In 1793, George Washington gave the shortest speech in 135 polite, if brief, words. In contrast, William Henry Harrison

weighed in with over 8,000 words in 1841.

The new President Obama had nothing either so long or short in mind. He hoped to strike a note of confidence in the

future even as the country was dealing with the toughest problems it had faced in generations. Barack wanted to remind Americans that no problem is too big to overcome if they all work together. This was not a moment for despair.

"On this day, we gather because we have chosen hope over fear, unity of purpose over conflict and discord," he said. "On this

President Obama delivers his inaugural address in Washington DC.

83

day, we come to proclaim an end to the petty grievances and false promises... Starting today, we must pick ourselves up, dust ourselves off, and begin again the work of remaking America."

And President Obama had thoughts to share with his global audience. "From the grandest capitals to the small village where my father was born: know that America is a friend of each nation and every man, woman, and child who seeks a future of peace and dignity, and we are ready to lead once more."

As Barack Obama finished speaking, a wave of applause rang out. Millions of people had come to witness this moment. The president's inauguration was watched on television and heard on the radio all over the world. Kenya declared a national holiday in Barack's honour.

One immediate change that came with the Obama White House was the presence of children. Malia, ten, and Sasha, seven, were the first children to live there since nine-year-old Amy Carter, daughter of President Jimmy Carter in 1976. Barack had promised his daughters a pet

dog, and Senator Ted Kennedy, the brother
of former president, John F. Kennedy, gave the
Obamas a Portuguese water dog named Bo.

It was helpful that Barack no longer had
to commute to Chicago to see his children,
because there was serious work to be done.
There were wars in Iraq and Afghanistan, and
long-standing uncertainties in the Middle East.
During his first months as president, Barack
was keen to show the world that the US would
work with other countries on major issues. And
for his efforts in bringing nations together,
Barack won the Nobel Peace Prize in 2009.

There was also the problem of a global financial crisis. Barack decided that the government would support the economy with a huge injection of money. Some of this money would go to support companies that wouldn't be able to exist without it. This kind of support had never been attempted on so large a scale, and there was no guarantee it would work. However, it did, and the country's economy was able to gradually recover over the next few years.

Another major challenge facing Barack was health care. Millions of US citizens had no support if they got sick. While people over the age of sixty-five were covered by health insurance, younger people had no such protection. President Obama planned to change that situation with the Affordable Care Act. Obamacare, as it came to be known, was a plan to provide people with coverage for illnesses and surgeries along with regular check-ups to keep them in good health. Some politicians did not agree with the plan, but the act became law in March 2010.

The most emotional event of Obama's first term came on 2 May 2011. Osama Bin Laden, the mastermind behind the devastating 9/11 attacks that had taken place in the United States ten years earlier, was killed during a raid on a housing compound in Pakistan. His death provided a kind of closure that had been missing while he was still at large.

9/11

On September 11, 2001, terrorist attacks in New York City and other parts of the US took the lives of almost 3,000 people. The tragedy unfolded as two hijacked passenger aircraft were flown directly into the twin towers of the World Trade Center in Manhattan, New York City.

The World Trade Center Memorial

President Obama and his top advisers watching the attack on Osama Bin Laden's hideout on live stream video on 1 May 2011.

A more positive note was reached with the appointment of two women, Elena Kagan and Sonia Sotomayor, to the US Supreme Court. Up until then, the Supreme Court had never had more than two female justices, or judges. Now, along with Ruth Bader Ginsburg, there were three. There was hope that a time would come when appointing a new female justice would be so common it wouldn't be news at all.

In the mid-term elections in 2010, Republicans took back control of the House of Representatives, and after that, it became more difficult for Barack Obama and the Democrats to achieve any major goals, because the House of Representatives under Republican leadership would not support them. It was a sign of things to come that they could not find much room to achieve any positive agreements for the rest of President Obama's first term.

Justice Ruth Bader Ginsburg was a great campaigner for women's rights and gender equality.

Sonia Sotomayor has served as a justice since 2009.

Elena Kagan became justice in 2010.

11

A second term

There was never any real question of whether President Obama was going to run for a second term.

He believed he had more work to do. And even if the battles ahead would be uphill ones, he was not going to shrink from fighting them.

There were questions, though, about which Republican candidate he would be running against. As things turned out, his opponent was Mitt Romney, a moderate Republican and former governor of Massachusetts. His running mate was Congressman Paul Ryan from Wisconsin.

Romney and Ryan tried to make the case that they were better suited to lead the country through the ongoing financial recovery. But since the recovery itself was already under way and going well, it was hard for this claim to win people over.

ELECTORAL COLLEGE

At the presidential level, candidates are not elected as a direct result of the national popular vote. Instead, their victory or loss in each state determines who will get that state's Electoral College votes. (The number of Electoral College votes in each state is the sum of their Senate and congressional representatives.) Although it has only happened a few times, it is possible for a candidate to lose the popular vote and still be elected president if the votes fall the right way in enough states.

They then attempted to paint President Obama as leading a government that was interfering in ordinary people's business. However, this approach also failed to improve their position. The election was no landslide, but with a victory in the popular vote and the Electoral College, it was still a decisive win for Barack Obama as president and Joe Biden as vice president.

Barack Obama with Joe Biden

CLIMATE CHANGE

Perhaps the greatest crisis facing the world today is the changing climate. This has been brought about by the release of harmful gases into the atmosphere, mainly caused by the burning of fossil fuels. These emissions have led to a gradual rising of temperatures worldwide, which in turn has resulted in the melting of polar ice caps and the rise of sea levels. This change poses a huge threat to the way we live and it will not end without help from countries across the world.

As Republicans in Congress continued to block any attempts to make headway on domestic issues, President Obama went abroad looking to make progress. The effects of climate change had become increasingly evident across the globe, and a meeting was held in Paris, France, in the spring of 2015 to address this concern. The result was the Paris Climate Accord, in which the United States was a leading participant. It was a major achievement of Obama's second term. This agreement sought to limit global warming by regulating greenhouse gas emissions, and it was eventually signed by 196 countries.

After the 2014 election returned the Senate to Republican control, it became very difficult for the Obama administration to achieve much of anything that required congressional cooperation. Republicans were intent on biding their time, hoping that the next presidential election would put them back in control of both Congress and the White House.

In 2015, President Obama addressed the United Nations Climate Change Conference – COP21.

One highlight of the second term was Obama's participation in the 50th anniversary of the Civil Rights March in Alabama. This groundbreaking march had taken place in 1965, and was led by Dr Martin Luther King, Jr. The participants had been protesting against the roadblocks that were enforcing segregation and making it difficult or even impossible for Black people to vote in some states.

A few months later President Lyndon Johnson had signed the Civil Rights Act that took major steps towards restoring a number of rights to Black Americans.

In another speech three years later, King had famously said that "the arc of the moral universe is long. But it bends toward justice".

In the anniversary march, President Obama made reference to this idea, while adding, "The arc of the universe may bend toward justice, but it doesn't bend on its own."

DID YOU KNOW?

Martin Luther King, Jr skipped two grades at school and entered Morehead College at the age of fifteen.

DR MARTIN LUTHER KING, JR

Born in 1929, Martin Luther King, Jr was at the forefront of the
Civil Rights Movement in the United States during the 1950s and
1960s. This was the struggle to gain equal rights for all Black
Americans under US law. King won the Nobel Peace Prize in
1964 for campaigning for civil rights through non-violent
means. His work led to the groundbreaking Civil Rights Act of
1965. Tragically, in 1968 Martin Luther King, Jr was assassinated
in Memphis, Tennessee, at the age of 39.

In 1965, Dr Martin Luther King, Jr (centre) led civil rights protestors on their five-day march from Selma to Montgomery in Alabama.

In 2015, President Obama and First Lady Michelle Obama led the walk across the Edmund Pettus Bridge in Selma to commemorate the 50th anniversary of the Civil Rights March.

For the remainder of his second term,
Obama's achievements were largely met outside
the reach of Congress. His two earlier additions
to the Supreme Court had helped to establish the
Court's decision to recognize the right to same-sex
marriage nationwide. With the approval of the
Federal Communications Commission, he
also was able to put $8 billion dollars towards
increasing Internet access for lower-income rural
families. By 2016, 98 per cent of all Americans
had access to faster Internet speeds.

There was a bittersweet aspect to the end of the term itself, however. Although Obama had not found himself weighed down by any significant personal or political scandals, it was hard to escape the feeling that some people didn't like him. At the 2016 Democratic Convention, his wife Michelle had famously said in reference to bullies, "when they go low, we go high".

Barack Obama fulfilled many of his dreams when he was elected president. Some of them were his own, of course, but many other people had shared in those dreams as well.

Chapter

12

Next steps

Former presidents have a lot of choices when it comes to how to spend their time after they leave office.

George Washington was eager to retire to his estate at Mount Vernon and resume his life as a gentlemen farmer. John Quincy Adams returned to Massachusetts and became a congressman. William Howard Taft became Chief Justice of the United States Supreme Court.

Whatever his immediate plans, Barack Obama was not planning to just fade away. He was firmly convinced that democracy and the United States remained a work in progress. As he said in his Farewell Address on 10 January 2017: "Understand, democracy does not require uniformity. Our founders quarrelled and compromised, and expected us

to do the same. But they knew that democracy does require a basic sense of solidarity – the idea that for all our outward differences, we are all in this together; that we rise or fall as one."

Clearly, the soon-to-be-retired president planned to participate in that ongoing mission. But how should he begin? For Barack Obama, who at fifty-five became one of the youngest former presidents who had served two terms, it was only natural that he would remain busy in many ways. The first thing he decided to do was not to move away. This was unusual – no president had done this since Woodrow Wilson in 1920. The Obamas decided to stay in

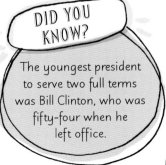

DID YOU KNOW?

The youngest president to serve two full terms was Bill Clinton, who was fifty-four when he left office.

Washington for a very good reason. They wanted their younger daughter Sasha to be able to finish her high school education at Sidwell Friends School, where she was in the middle of her sophomore, or second year.

As far as sharing their personal stories were concerned, both Barack and Michelle Obama signed contracts to publish their memoirs. Michelle's book, *Becoming*, was published in November 2018. Having since sold more than 10 million copies, it has established itself as one of the most successful memoirs of all time. Two years later, the first volume of Barack's

MEMOIRS

Memoirs are a kind of autobiography usually focusing on particular periods in the person's life rather than giving a complete record starting from birth.

Michelle's memoir, *Becoming*

Barack's memoir, *A Promised Land*

planned two-volume memoir, *A Promised Land*, was published to great success as well.

Although Barack has largely followed the presidential tradition of staying out of the spotlight, he made one of his most prominent public appearances speaking at the funeral of one of his heroes, the congressman and civil rights leader, John Lewis. A dedicated politician and legendary activist, Lewis was someone who never stopped fighting for justice. Barack could only hope to make as much of a difference as his idol, and it was an honour to speak in his memory.

John Lewis

One ongoing focus for the former president has been encouraging people, both young and old, to vote. Voting is important because it is the first step on the road to political progress. "I'm hopeful," he said in 2018, "that despite all the noise, all the lies, we're going to remember who we are, who we're called to be. Out of this political darkness, I see a great awakening. If you vote, things will get better, it will be a start."

Barack means "one who is blessed" in Swahili. This courageous politician has never been one to dwell on the shortcomings of the past or the disappointments of the present and he remains hopeful and optimistic even in the face of adversity. As Barack once remarked, "The future rewards those who press on. I don't have time to feel sorry for myself. I don't have time to complain. I'm going to press on."

109

Obama's **family tree**

Malik Obama
1958–

Half-brother father's side

Auma Obama
1960–

Half-sister father's side

Mark Okoth Obama Ndesandjo
1965–

Half-brother father's side

David Ndesandjo
1968–1987

Half-brother father's side

Wife

Michelle Obama
1964–

Malia Obama
1998–

Daughter

Sasha Obama
2001–

Daughter

Father

Barack Hussein
Obama Senior
1936–1982

Mother

Ann Dunham
1942–1995

George Hussein
Onyango Obama
1982–

Half-brother
father's side

Maya
Soetoro-Ng
1970–

Half-sister
mother's side

Barack Hussein
Obama
1961–

111

Timeline

Ann files for divorce from Barack Obama Sr.

Barack Hussein Obama is born in Honolulu, Hawaii, to Barack Obama Sr and Ann Dunham.

Barack returns to Hawaii where he lives with his grandparents, Stanley and Madelyn Dunham.

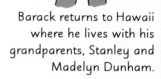

1961   1962   1964   1967   1971

Barack Obama Sr moves to Massachusetts to attend Harvard University without Ann and Barack.

Barack's mother, Ann, marries Lolo Soetoro and they all move to Indonesia.

Barack attends
Occidental College
in Los Angeles,
California.

Barack transfers to
Columbia University
in New York to study
political science.

Barack makes a
career breakthrough
and moves to Chicago
to begin work as a
community organizer.

1979　1981　1983　1985　1988

Barack attends Harvard
Law School in Cambridge,
Massachusetts, in an effort
to be more able to help
people as a lawyer.

Barack graduates from
Columbia University and
takes a job as a researcher for
a company in New York City.

Barack is elected as the first ever African American president of the *Harvard Law Review*.

Michelle Obama gives birth to the couple's first child, a girl, Malia.

Barack Obama and Michelle Robinson are married at the Trinity United Church of Christ in Chicago.

Barack's mother, Ann, passes away after battling with cancer.

1990   1991   1992   1995   1996   1998

Barack's memoir, *Dreams from My Father*, is published.

Barack is elected as state senator in Chicago's South Side.

Having graduated from Harvard, Barack returns to Chicago to begin work as a civil rights lawyer.

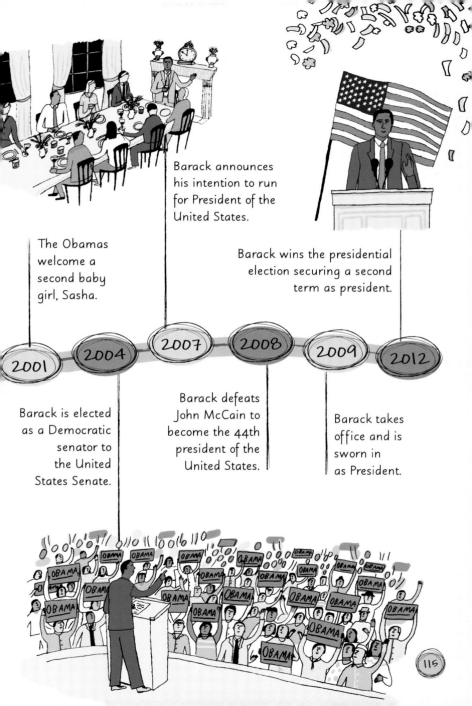

Barack announces his intention to run for President of the United States.

The Obamas welcome a second baby girl, Sasha.

Barack wins the presidential election securing a second term as president.

2001 2004 2007 2008 2009 2012

Barack is elected as a Democratic senator to the United States Senate.

Barack defeats John McCain to become the 44th president of the United States.

Barack takes office and is sworn in as President.

Quiz

 Who did Barack live with in Hawaii while his mum and sister were still in Indonesia?

 What sport did Barack spend a lot of time playing when he returned to Hawaii?

 What major racial issue did Barack speak passionately about while at college in Los Angeles?

 What was Barack's first job after he graduated from Columbia University?

 In what city did Barack start his job as a community organizer?

 What was the title of the church sermon that Barack listened to that brought him to tears?

 What aspect of law was Michelle Robinson a specialist in?

Did you enjoy the book? Show us what you know!

 What was the name of the law journal that Barack became president of?

 What was the name of the book that Barack published in 1995?

 What was the name of the US congressman who defeated Barack in the 2000 election?

 Who did Barack beat to become the Democratic nominee for president?

 Who did Barack beat in the 2008 presidential election to become president of the United States?

Answers on page 128

Who's who?

Biden, Joe
(1942–) vice president in Obama's government from 2009 to 2017; he became president of the US in 2021

Bush, George W.
(1946–) president of the US from 2001 to 2009

Clinton, Bill
(1946–) president of the US from 1993 to 2001

Clinton, Hillary
(1947–) First Lady when her husband Bill Clinton was president (1993–2001); she served as Secretary of State in Barack's government from 2009–2013 and was a US senator and Democratic nominee for president of the US in 2016

Dunham, Ann
(1942–1995) Barack's mother and role model. She worked as an anthropologist

Dunham, Madelyn
(1922–2008) Barack's grandmother who raised him, from age 10, in Hawaii, with Barack's grandfather

Dunham, Stanley
(1918–1992) Barack's grandfather who raised him, from age 10, in Hawaii, with Barack's grandmother

Kerry, John F.
(1943–) US senator and the Democratic nominee for president of the US in 2004. Kerry served as Secretary of State in Barack's government from 2013–2017

Lewis, John
(1940–2020) US statesman and civil rights activist; he served in the United States House of Representatives for Georgia's 5th congressional district from 1987–2020

McCain, John
(1936–2018) veteran of the Vietnam War and a US senator. He was the Republican nominee for president of the US in the 2008 election, losing to Barack Obama

Ndesandjo, David
(1968–1987) Barack's half-brother on his father's side

Obama, Auma
(1960–) Barack's half-sister on his father's side; she is a journalist, lecturer, and director of her own charitable foundation

Obama Sr, Barack
(1936–1982) Barack's father; he worked as an economist for the Kenyan government

Obama, Malia
(1998–) eldest daughter of Michelle and Barack

Obama, Sasha
(2001–) second, and youngest, daughter of Michelle and Barack

Palin, Sarah
(1964–) governor of Alaska and John McCain's choice to be vice president in the 2008 presidential election

Robinson, Michelle
(1964–) Barack's wife and mother of their two children; Michelle was First Lady

Romney, Mitt
(1947–) Republican nominee for president of the US in 2012

Rush, Bobby
(1946–) US congressman who defeated Barack in the 2000 election for US Congress

Soetoro, Lolo
(1935–1987) Barack's stepfather and second husband to his mother, Ann

Soetoro-Ng, Maya
(1970–) Barack's half-sister on his mother's side; Maya is an academic and teacher

Glossary

American Civil War
war fought between the North and South of the US (1861–1865) that resulted in the abolishment of slavery

American Revolution
war fought between Britain and its American colonies (1775–1783) that resulted in American independence

boycott
refusal to do something as a protest in the hope to bring about change

campus
area of land containing university or college buildings

candidate
person who puts themselves forward for a particular position or job

Christian
person who believes in Jesus Christ and his teachings

civil rights
rights that people have that ensure they are treated fairly and equally

corporate
relating to big business

corporation
big company or group of companies joined together

discriminatory
treating a person or group of people unfairly

diverse
people or objects that are different from one another

domestic
event or situation inside a particular country

ethnic
connection between a group of people based on racial or cultural similarities

grievance
belief that a person has been unfairly treated and so has cause to complain

heritage
part of a person's identity that is passed onto them because of their background and tradition

hijacked
illegally taking control of something, such as an aircraft, using force

housing compound
group of buildings used for the purpose of providing a home for people

identity
features of a person that make them who they are

inaugural
first speech given by a new leader, such as a president

injustice
outcome of a situation that is considered to be unfair

intern
person employed on a temporary basis

interracial
something that involves people of different races

landslide
huge victory in an election

middle class
social group that have a comfortable standard of living and social status

moderate
political opinion that is judged to be reasonable and not extreme

Muslim
person who believes in the religious teachings of Islam and follows its rules

nominee
someone who is put forward, or nominated, for a particular position or job within a political party

open seat
vacancy within government that arises when the current occupant does not intend to run for re-election

partisanship
support for a political decision or course of action in order to be loyal to the political party you belong to

prejudice
unfair dislike of a person or group of people often based on false information

privileged
person or group of people who have an advantage over most other people in society

professional
jobs that require a particular level of skill and education

racial
things to do with or that relate to race

racial discrimination
unfair treatment of a person or group of people because of their race

red tape
rules and procedures that needlessly hold up progress on particular issues

rickshaw
small two-wheeled passenger vehicle pulled by a person

scandal
event that is considered shocking and results in media attention and gossip

schedule
plan that outlines a list of events or tasks and when they should be completed by

solidarity
showing support for a person or a group of people who share a common belief

stock market
financial market where shares in money are traded

Supreme Court
highest court in the US responsible for ensuring laws follow the Constitution

three-pointer
points awarded in basketball for scoring beyond the three-point line

underprivileged
people who have less money and fewer opportunities than the majority of society

vice president
person in a government who is second in command to the president and who takes over if the president dies, is absent, or is replaced

working class
social group that generally work in manual or industrial jobs and receive lower pay

World War II
major war (1939–1945) that started in Europe and spread to other parts of the world

Index

Acknowledgements

DK would like to thank: Caroline Hunt for proofreading; Helen Peters for the index; Kieran Jones for writing the reference section
The author would like to thank his editor Marie Greenwood for both her good humour and attention to detail

Works cited:
p.11: "In many parts . . ." Barack Obama: *Dreams from My Father*, p.12.
p.12: "retrace the first steps. . ." ibid. p.23.
p.14: "dog meat . . ." ibid. p.31.
p.15: "This is no picnic . . ." ibid. p.48.
p.16: "they lived . . ." ibid. p.60.
p. 17: "to throw a football . . ." ibid. p.60.
p. 18 "any kind of cruelty . . ." Barack Obama: *The Audacity of Hope*, p.66.
p. 23: "I started . . ." ibid. p.67.
p. 35: "The drive-by . . ." *Dreams from My Father*, p.252.
p. 42: "I am telling . . ." ibid. p.336.
p. 43: "seemed to be . . ." ibid. p.299.
p. 43: "the well worn furniture . . ." ibid. p.290.
p. 44: "stone and . . ." ibid. p.319.
p. 44: "wildebeest, with . . ." ibid. p.321.
p. 45: "pink eyes and nostrils . . ." ibid. p.325.
p. 45: "their chins . . ." ibid. p.325
p. 45: "vultures watched . . ." ibid. p.325
p. 46 "Once upon . . ." ibid. p.339.
p. 46: "If I say . . ." ibid. p.340.
p. 52: "in my legal . . ." ibid. p.400.
p. 55: "Honesty, empathy . . ." Barack Obama: *The Audacity of Hope*, p.205.

p. 59: "The sort of . . ." ibid. p.3.
p. 61: "a lot of people . . ." (2004 *The New Yorker* profile)
p. 61: "I noticed that . . ." (2004 *The New Yorker* profile)
p. 63: "I am not . . ." (2004 *The New Yorker* profile)
p. 64: "most of them . . ." Barack Obama: *The Audacity of Hope*, p.7.
p. 65: "that we . . ." 2004 Democratic Convention keynote speech
p. 71: "Are you going . . ." Editors of LIFE: *The American Journey of Barack Obama*, p.123.
p. 81: "In this country . . ." 2008 acceptance speech
p. 83: "On this day . . ." 2009 Inaugural Address
p. 84: "From the grandest . . ." 2009 Inaugural Address
p. 96: "the arc of the moral . . ." obamawhitehouse.archives. gov
p. 96: "The arc of the universe . . ." 2013 Commemorative MLK Speech
p. 103: "when they . . ." 2016 Democratic Convention speech
p. 104: "Understand democracy . . ." Barack Obama, Farewell Address, 10 January 2017, obamawhitehouse.archives.gov
p. 107: "I'm hopeful . . ." 2018 Detroit campaign speech
p. 108: "The future rewards . . ." 2011 Congressional Black Caucus Dinner speech

ANSWERS TO THE QUIZ ON PAGES 116–117

1. his grandparents; 2. basketball; 3. apartheid; 4. a researcher;
5. Chicago; 6. The Audacity of Hope; 7. entertainment law;
8. the *Harvard Law Review*; 9. *Dreams from My Father*;
10. Bobby Rush; 11. Hillary Clinton; 12. John McCain